MW01644824

STRANDED

ISBN: 978-1-63813-361-2

Cover and interior design: Kristi Yoder

Cover art and interior illustrations: Laura Yoder

Printed in China

Published by:

CAM Books
P.O. Box 355
Berlin, Ohio 44610 USA
Phone: 330.893.4828
Fax: 330.893.4893
cambooks.org

STRANDED

Melinda Troyer

DEDICATION

This book is dedicated to Louise Shrock, who was the dearest and sweetest 100-year-old lady I have ever known! And to her daughters—Joanne, Jeanne, and Karen. God bless you!

INTRODUCTION

This true story took place near Ligonier, Indiana, on March 26, 1930.

Louise (Steury) Shrock, the main character, was born on October 4, 1922. She lived to be 100 years old and proved to be quite a prayer warrior in her old age. She died early on Thanksgiving Day in 2022.

Louise always cherished the lesson she learned during this blizzard—that even when people can't be with you, God is always present. He is always taking care of you.

This lesson stayed with her until the end of her life.

Chapter 1

STUCK!

"Look at it snow!" exclaimed six-year-old Louise Steury to her friend Lucille.

"Wow! You almost can't see the tree out by the road." Lucille stared out the schoolhouse window.

The boys rushed up, gazing in wonder at the fury of the storm. "I didn't wear my winter coat," said Clyde Becker, another first grader. He pressed his nose against the frosty windowpane.

When Mrs. Zook rang the bell, the children scampered to their seats. Louise tried to concentrate on her lessons, but she kept looking out at the white, white world. The snow swirled round and round, with gusts of wind blasting it into deep drifts. She shivered.

Mrs. Zook walked to the window. "That snow looks deep!" she exclaimed. "And it's getting deeper. We need to go home. Oh, I see the bus coming now, so you may get your coats."

Noisily the children got dressed. "I wish I had my thick coat," said one. "It was warm this morning!"

"I wish I had my boots!" said another.

Louise heard the comments but said nothing. *I wish I had my gloves and my boots and my thick coat,* she thought. *But at least I have my scarf. Most of the other girls don't even have that. What's going to happen to us?* She bit her lip.

As she stepped on the bus a few minutes later, she hesitated. *Where should I sit?* There were seats beside the windows on both sides of the bus, and a center seat ran down the middle of the bus. It had no backrest, so a person could sit facing either way.

Usually Louise sat in the middle seat, but not today. *If I sit by the window, I can look outside.*

"Take your seat, Missy." Burl Conrad, the bus driver, smiled at her.

Louise's brother Virgil pushed her shoulder. "Hurry up."

Louise dropped into a seat and stared outside at the swirling white

curtain. *How can we get home in this blizzard? Are we going to be all right?* The other students jostled each other and stomped the snow off their feet as they got settled.

Clyde Becker sat in the middle seat, facing her. “Who’s that man?” he asked, nodding at a tall man sitting behind the driver.

“I don’t know,” Louise replied.

With a lurch, the bus started off and chugged through the heavy snow. Every time they stopped and opened the door to let out students, the bus got cold. Then the bus slowed down again, and Louise heard the motor labor. Her heart raced and her mouth felt dry. *What's going to happen?*

The bus stopped.

"Uh, oh," said the stranger.

"I'll back up and rev the motor," Burl said. He backed up the bus and tried again, but the vehicle shuddered to a halt.

“We’ll have to shovel.” The stranger pulled on his gloves.

Burl opened the door and a blast of cold air hit Louise. She shivered.

Thumps, thuds, and scraping sounds came from outside. Louise’s tummy hurt. *How will we get home?*

The minutes dragged by. At last the two men came back in. The engine roared and the bus shook, but it did not move. Not one inch.

“We have to shovel more,” commented Burl to his helper.

The children could hear more scrapes, thumps, and thuds outside as the men shoveled. It was getting cold, and Louise could see her breath. Her hands felt icy. *Will we freeze?*

Finally the two men entered the bus, and Burl gunned the motor again. *Vroom! Vroom!* But though the engine roared and the bus shook, it did not move.

Burl turned off the engine and stood up. His cap brushed the ceiling. He motioned to his helper. "We need to carry the two youngest to the closest farm."

Turning to Thad Stoltz, the oldest boy on the bus, Burl said, "Keep everyone on the bus. Do not let anyone get off. That drift outside is waist deep for the little ones. We'll come back for you, but it will take a while."

He peered at Louise and Clyde, the two first graders. "Come." He picked up Louise in his fatherly arms, while his helper picked up Clyde.

A blast of icy wind hit Louise's face the instant they were out

of the bus. She turned her face toward Burl and snuggled closer, trying to avoid the frigid air. Her bare hands felt numb, and her feet were like blocks of ice.

Chapter 2

HOME AWAY FROM HOME

The trek went on and on. Louise began to feel sleepy. Finally they entered a house and Louise recognized where they were—at Robert Wolf's house. And Robert was still on the bus.

The bus driver put her down. "This girl is from the Amish family that just moved into the area."

The warmth felt wonderful. Louise wanted to run to the stove, but Robert's mom stopped her.

"Wait, child!" she exclaimed. "Your hands are almost frozen!" Fetching a dishpan of fresh snow, she plunged Louise's stiff white hands into it and began massaging them. She also took off Louise's shoes and rubbed snow on her icy cold feet.

"No . . ." whimpered Louise. Tears rolled down her cheeks. Why didn't Mrs. Wolf let her run to the stove and warm her hands? Pain shot through her hands and feet. She cried out in agony as Mrs. Wolf

continued to rub snow on them.

Louise didn't notice when the men left, but a long time later she heard them coming back.

The room filled with boys and girls from the school bus, stomping their feet and shaking snow off their clothes. Everyone crowded close to the stove. Louise saw her brother Virgil. Just seeing his smile helped her feel calmer inside.

He stepped close to her and looked at her hands. "Does it hurt a lot?" he asked.

Louise blinked back the tears. “Yes, it hurts,” she choked out. “My feet hurt too.”

At suppertime, Louise’s hands burned like fire. She whimpered when she tried to pick up a spoon.

Naomi, a neighbor lady who had come to help, gently took the spoon and fed her.

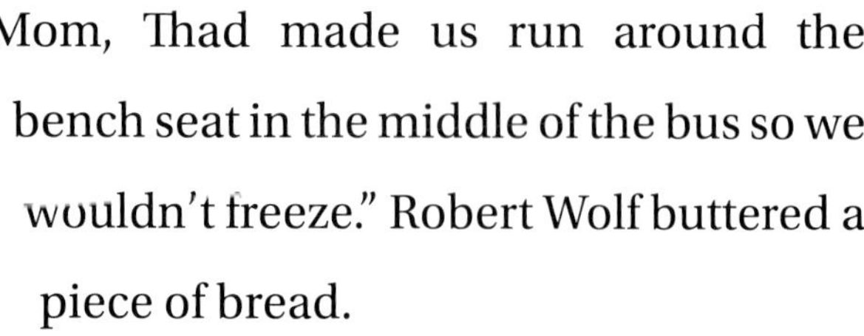

“Mom, Thad made us run around the bench seat in the middle of the bus so we wouldn’t freeze.” Robert Wolf buttered a piece of bread.

Louise’s brother Virgil looked at Burl. “I was really glad to see that bobsled with the horses. I thought we might freeze.”

“Yes, it was good that Mr. Wolf had a bobsled we could use.” Burl sipped his coffee. “We had to come through the field because the snowdrifts on the road were too deep for the horses.”

“Those thick blankets on the sled felt wonderful,” Ruth, one of the older girls, commented.

“We didn’t freeze. You took good care of us, Dad.” Russel Conrad nodded at Burl, his dad.

After supper, someone knocked on the door. Louise looked up. *Who could be out in this storm?*

Mr. Wolf opened the door. “Come in! Come in! Get out of the cold!” he said.

Louise saw her dad, Victor Steury, with several of their neighbors. She darted to Dad, wrapped her arms around him, and began to cry.

“There. There. You’re okay.” Dad’s firm hands patted her back. “Mom and I were really concerned, so the neighbor men and I walked the bus route until we found the bus stuck in the snow.”

“I want to go home with you,” begged Louise, clinging to him.

Dad picked her up and held her close. “Louise, you would freeze! Your hands look frostbitten now. Just wait here with Virgil, and I’ll come get you with our bobsled when the storm is over.”

"The radio said we have a forty-mile-an-hour wind out there and eighteen inches of snow," a neighbor man said. "The drifts are several feet high!"

"My wife was out in the garden yesterday," another neighbor said. "This is hard to believe!"

“But, Daddy, I’m sc-scared,” whispered Louise.

Dad squatted down beside her and cupped her cheeks in his big hands. “I understand. But listen. God is always with you. Jesus said, ‘Lo, I am with you always.’ God is only a prayer away, and He is a good Father. Mom and I will pray for you.”

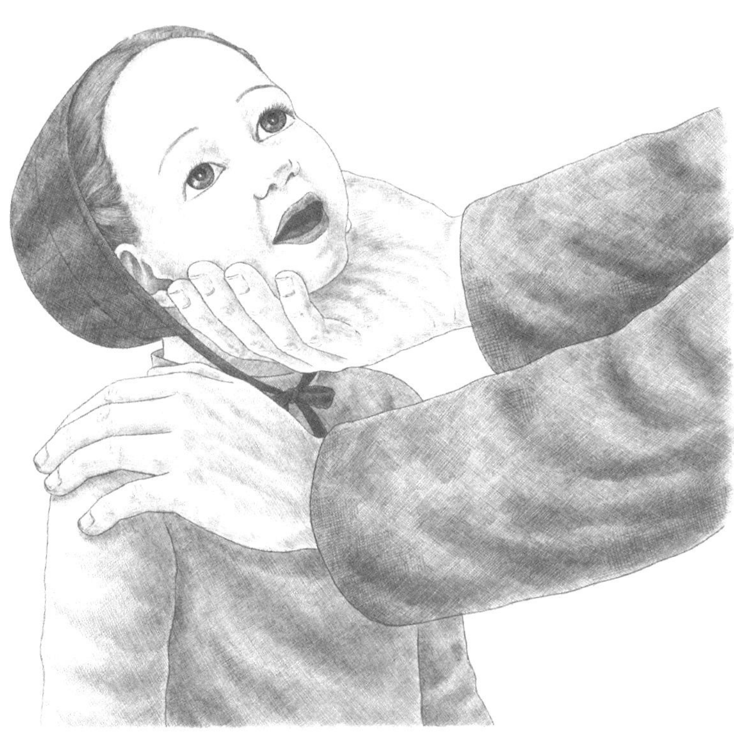

After the men left, Mrs. Wolf gathered blankets for beds. As Mrs. Wolf tucked her in for the night, Louise began to cry. “I want to go home,” she said.

“Hush, child,” Mrs. Wolf said, trying to soothe her.

Louise just cried harder.

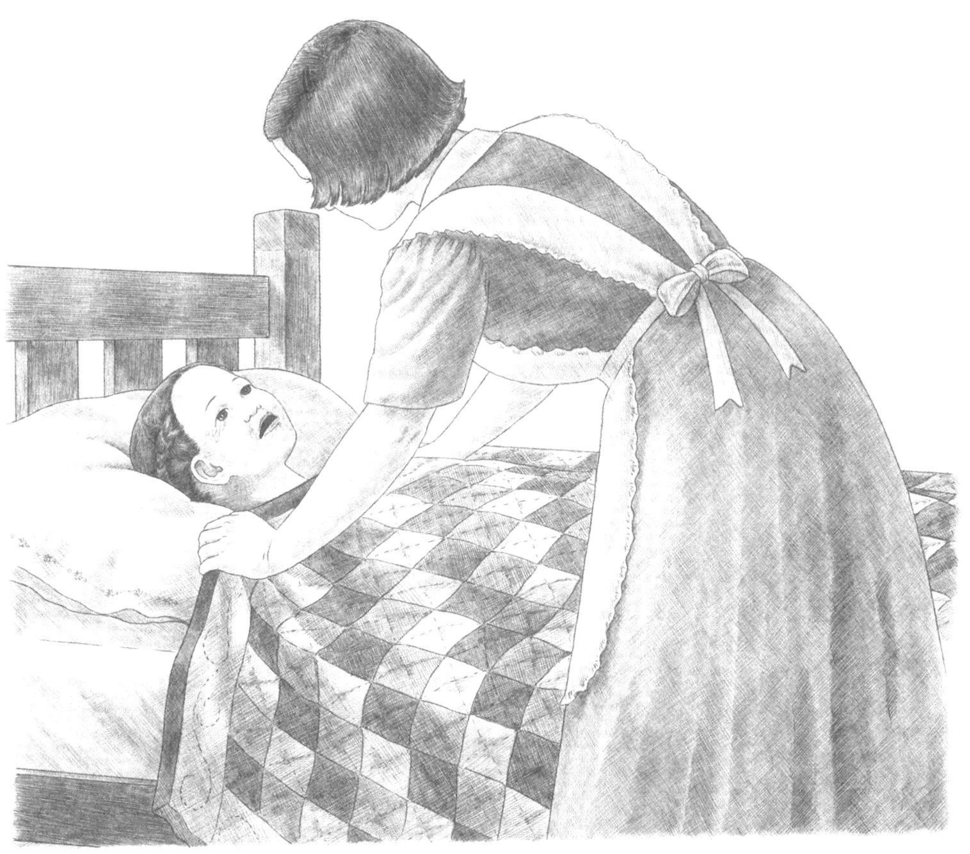

At last Mrs. Wolf stepped to the door and motioned for Virgil to come.

Her brother tucked the blankets around her. "Don't be afraid," he whispered in her ears. "I'm stuck here too. Let me pray with you."

Louise relaxed as Virgil prayed. She would be all right. Her brother was here, and God was watching over her.

Chapter 3

HOME AGAIN

The wind and snow died down during the night, and the sun shone brightly the next morning. *Now I can go home!* Louise thought. She breathed deeply in relief.

"But you can't go right away," explained Mrs. Wolf as she helped Louise put on her covering. "The men need to open the roads first."

Her swollen hands still hurt, so once again someone fed her at breakfast time. But things weren't as frightening as the night before. The children laughed and giggled.

Later that morning, Louise stood at the window and stared with open-mouthed wonder. The snowdrift came up to the top of the fence! She saw Mr. Wolf shoveling a path to the barn. The snow on both sides of the path came to his shoulders. But in other places, the ground was almost bare.

The stay at the Wolf farm was becoming fun. An adventure.

Louise saw Ruth ask Mrs. Wolf for a button. "Okay," said Ruth. "Let's play 'Button, button, who's got the button?' Virgil, you can be 'it' first."

The children used the stair steps to sit on to play the game. Louise noticed that she and Virgil were the only Amish children there, but it didn't matter. She felt her shoulders relax as she joined in the giggles and the games.

Just before lunchtime they saw men shoveling the drift away, clearing the road. *Now Dad can get through! I can't wait!*

Sure enough, after lunch Dad drove in with the big bobsled pulled by sturdy workhorses. The bobsled was filled with straw and thick blankets.

"All aboard!" cried Dad. "I will take you all to your homes. Make sure you get your lunch pails and books. Don't leave anything here."

He looked at Louise and said, "How did it go? Did you find God's promise true?"

Louise nodded her head. God had indeed been with her.

Happy, chattering children hopped on the sled, eager to go home.

As Dad clicked his tongue to tell the horses to start, Louise looked around. Her friends jabbered cheerily beside her, and the snow crunched underneath the sled. The fresh snow glittered like a million diamonds in the sunshine. She took a deep, deep breath. She was going home at last!

She had learned that although Mom and Daddy could not always be with her, it was all right. God was there.

She smiled all the way to her toes.

ABOUT THE AUTHOR

Melinda Troyer lives in northern Indiana near Shipshewana.

She has always enjoyed reading, and even in school she loved writing stories. She has successfully finished several writing courses for The Institute of Children's Literature and has had over 200 short stories published.

She works as a caregiver, taking care of the elderly in their homes.

She would love to hear from you! You may write to her in care of Christian Aid Ministries, P.O. Box 360, Berlin, OH 44610.

ABOUT CHRISTIAN AID MINISTRIES

Christian Aid Ministries was founded in 1981 as a nonprofit, tax-exempt 501(c)(3) organization. Its primary purpose is to provide a trustworthy and efficient channel for Amish, Mennonite, and other conservative Anabaptist groups and individuals to minister to physical and spiritual needs around the world. This is in response to the command to "Do good unto all men, especially unto them who are of the household of faith" (Galatians 6:10).

CAM supporters provide millions of pounds of food, clothing, Bibles, medicines, and other aid each year. Supporters' funds also help victims of disasters in the U.S. and abroad, put up Gospel billboards in the U.S., and provide Biblical teaching and self-help resources. CAM's main purposes for providing aid are to help and encourage God's people and bring the Gospel to a lost and dying world.